# As We Carry On

# by

# Mary Jo Brinkley

An RGMD Media Inc. Publication - Rockwall, Texas

AS WE CARRY ON
by Mary Jo Brinkley

**Mary Jo Brinkley**
1717 Castle Drive
Garland, Texas 75040

**ISBN:**  978-0-9828784-0-8

Front & Back Cover design: Pastor Glynn Davis
Layout & Formatting: Pastor Glynn Davis
Editing & Proofing: Lana Tydlaska


An RGMD Media Inc. Publication - Rockwall, Texas
Published for **Mary Jo Brinkley** by:
Jostens Commercial Publications
401 Science Park Road
State College, PA 16803
mccoym@uplink.net
Mike McCoy - 570-594-4957
www.jostens.com
Toll-free (878) 897-9693
Fax (717) 935-2283

Printed in the United States of America
Published January 2011

# Dedicated To My Grandchildren

**Luke, Michael, Matthew, Aimee, and Emma Grace**

*In Loving Memory Of*
*My beloved Albert*
*(Al Baby)*

*Special Thanks To*
*Pastors Glynn & Carolyn Davis*
*For Believing In Me*
*And This Book*

# Endorsements

From the time Mary Jo Brinkley was sitting on the front pew in her grandfather's church, she has been seeking the Lord. This quest shows in all that she has done as school secretary and friend for decades.

She meets each new challenge by asking what God would have her do. Often she is able to see humor in the chaos that ensues when we try to "run things" instead of letting God be God. This ability to laugh with life has made her an invaluable friend and counselor to those around her. She has prayed, cried, and laughed with me many times.

Mary Jo has written this book to teach, guide, and comfort her new friends; the readers. Enjoy the trip through the life of a woman who truly "walks with God."

**Juana Petkovsek**
Master Reading Teacher
Dallas ISD


I was a teenager when I first met Mary Jo Brinkley. She has always been a pillar of faith, a passionate woman of God, and has spoken such powerful words of support and love into my life. I've personally been blessed by her testimonies and faith.

Now the world can have access to this inspiration through this collection of short stories and real life accounts. Mary Jo will have you laughing, crying, and rejoicing within minutes.

You'll find her infectious personality captured in the pages of this wonderful book. Sit back and enjoy God's gift in Mary Jo the way many of us have for years. Thank you Mary Jo for making a difference in this teenager's life. May this book be just as big of a blessing as you've been to me.

**David Butler**
Associate Pastor
Abundant Life Church
Garland, Texas

I have known Mary Jo since we were teenagers in the early 1960's. We became such close friends at once. She introduced me to the love of my life, my husband Paul.

Mary Jo sees the gifts in others. She has experiences, adventures, and unique insights that loudly speak, (in her words) "carry on, do not give up on yourself."

Mary Jo is an awesome woman of God and I know that this book is inspired of our Lord. Her stories of the driving lessons, and other times she has had to grab hold of hope and faith will bless you.

**Edith Underwood**
First Lady, wife of Pastor Paul Underwood
Healton, Oklahoma

Mary Jo Brinkley has something to say to your heart within the pages of this book. I was introduced to the Brinkley family about ten years ago at Abundant Life Church.

One could not help but notice how close this family is. Some words that come to mind that best describe Mary Jo are: intercessor, teacher, wife, mother, caring, faithful, and humorous. (Now a widow of two years)

All of these go together to make up real Christian character. She studies the living stories of others to learn and grow from. You can clearly see Mary Jo's love for the Lord and the work of God! She has a love and excitement for people, and we who encounter her are never the same. She is devoted to her family and they are to her as well.

I would say Mary Jo is steadfast, unmovable always abounding in the work of the Lord. I am glad I know her and her family. As you read this book, you and I will cry, laugh, and rekindle our hope.

**Tonya Samples**
Prayer Pastor
Abundant Life Church
Garland, Texas

I have known Mary Jo Brinkley for over 15 years. Loving, caring, friendly, meticulous, and religious best describes this fine lady. I had the privilege of working with her as well as being her friend for over five years.

Mary Jo was the Office Manager for the elementary school where I served as principal. One of her major responsibilities centered around managing the school budget. She was the best! I never worried about accounts payable or activity accounts balancing. The pride and accuracy with which Mary Jo performed her duties was not likened by any other person in her postion. She was highly respected and admired. My office ran smoothly and efficiently all the time.

The same repertoire of attributes and characteristics Mary Jo displayed in the work place are in her home every single day. She manages her personal life with the same tenacity as her professional life.

The one characteristic I always admired was her undeniable deep religious faith and conviction. There was never a doubt that her religious beliefs were the thread that helped weave the attitude and actions of her daily life.

This characteristic never faltered, though certainly tested, even when her husband became gravely ill. She accepted it as God's will, and I believe, as a test of her faith.

She is a strong woman and through her examples has made others accept challenges and heartbreaking situations in their lives. Her attitude has already remained positive and this transcends to all she meets. I am proud to call her my friend!

**Judie Klaus**
Retired Principal
Dallas Independent School District

Reader's Digest for many years has had a monthly article entitled: "My Most Unforgettable Character." If I were able to write a book about special and unforgettable people, Mary Jo Brinkley would certainly be on that list. Having known the Brinkley family for over 25 years has been one of the great joys of our lives.

To say that Mary Jo is unique is a great understatement. Her love for God, her family, and friends is a wonderful example to us all. The legacy being handed down in this book to her family and close friends is amazing. Our prayer is that each member of the Brinkley family will treasure this gift as something priceless. Mary Jo is full of life and excitement and all of us who have the privilege to know her are the better for it!

She has been a joy to pastor and we have counted her and

Albert as dear friends.

She is a worshipper of our Lord Jesus Christ, a teacher of the Word of God, and a lady of faith.

Mary Jo, thank you for entrusting this manuscript to me for the layout, design, and formatting. I have done my best to handle your life's story with the dignity it deserves.

Thank you for being part of our lives, and thank you for protecting your heritage, and so freely passing it on to the next generation. We love you dearly.

**Glynn & Carolyn Davis**
Senior Pastors
Abundant Life Church
Garland, Texas

# Table Of Contents

# As We Carry On

# As We Carry On

This book of short stories, or chapters, is to share some of my story and of others' stories. This is only a glimpse into their story. A moment in time of a life that has impact!

The first few chapters are about my maternal grandparents who helped raise me. The remaining stories are about people and happenings either in my life or people that I have known. The title of this book I hope will become clear to you as you read the book.

I pray you will be blessed and know just how much that our Lord is faithful to His children. Faithful when we are crying or laughing. Faithful when we are young and when we are old. He is faithful so; carry on.

**Mary Jo Brinkley**
July 2010

# 1

# The Merry Go Round And The Lemonade

John Kelly, a young 19 year old Irish and German lad from Indiana was in Fort Smith, Arkansas to work in 1909. He was staying with his cousin. Bill showed the lad many things about the lumber mill where they worked. He, as well, took John to the lights of Ft. Smith. Bill delighted in seeing him experience life (as Bill knew life). John had been raised by Godly parents, so this was a new world for him.

John and Bill were the same age, and both had lost their dads. John was the oldest in his family, therefore he had to earn his way.

Summer was hot, and the Fourth of July this year was going to be special. Bill and John went to the fair grounds, so they could enjoy the celebrations. They arrived; children were running all over; laughing and playing. John went off to himself. He went over to where the ground's rides were. He found the merry go round. John saw a girl, then asked himself, "Was that a dream? She was real indeed. She had satin skin, green eyes and flaming red hair. She was holding a ribbon, where she had won the third place in the local beauty contest.

John got up on one of the ponies and introduced himself to the young lady. After some time of him rambling on, she told him her name was Nellie Peck. He asked her would she like some lemonade. Her answer, "Mr. Kelly, I would love to have some lemonade and ride this merry go round all afternoon." He went and bought up all the tickets he had money for. During the long ride they began to talk.

John began to call on Miss Nellie, and they fell deeply in love. A love that would last 60 years. He asked her uncle, (since her dad, was gone also) for her hand in marriage. First the uncle and her mother stated no because she was only 15 years old and he was poor. Nellie pleaded and told them she would run off and never come back. After many crying spells her family actually gave in.

They were married, on Sept. 12, 1909, in Van Buren, Arkansas, in a lovely old vine covered church. During the wedding, it came a rain storm. It rained and rained. John's white satin shirt was dripping wet by the time they got to her uncle's house for the reception.

John worked hard to become a good husband, and Nellie had to struggle to learn how to clean, cook and do all the things she had not had to do before.

Four years later and two daughters, the couple began to feel a strong need for their daughters to be raised in a church upbringing. They found a community church. They became a real part of that church. God called John to teach and preach the Word of God.

Thus, their ministry began. It would go through many battles, storms, and many victories. This was their precious love story. They both told it to me, after the many times I would ask them to do so. Thank God, for the merry go round and the lemonade...!

# 2

## Nellie To The Other Shore

John and Nellie Kelly had three girls and were expecting a fourth child as they moved to Buffalo, Iowa, (near Davenport). John had began to teach a Sunday School class. He went to work, for a cement company. They obtained a cute little house. Nellie was content to their settled and pleasant lives.

One night working an extra shift, a co-worker/friend, Jessie Charles and John were talking. Jessie told him about a woman preacher and her husband that were in Davenport. They had just came from the Azusa Street Revival in California. John asked were they fake. "No, they're not fake," was the answer. "John Kelly, they have had miracles happen in their services, which I saw with my own eyes."

"I am going to see for myself," thought John. I'll check out what the newspaper said about them. Time passed and then one day, as John was leaving work, Jessie came over to where John was. Jessie said, "I went again to the tent meetings I told you about. When you are there it is like being in the middle of the book of Acts." John went home and told Nellie what Jessie had said to him. She became scared. She wanted John to not have any part of these folks.

The tent revival in Davenport was the talk all over the planet. Jessie came in telling about his wife getting healed, just like in the Bible times. John Kelly became interested. He had a sister that dealt with pain daily. He wondered why this happened in the Bible, but in their church they were told it could not happen anymore.

On a Thursday evening, another worker got close to John and whispered to him that he had gotten saved and he received the Holy Spirit. John said, "That does it! I want to find out about this. Is it fake or real?"

John told Nellie he was going that weekend to those tent meetings. She begged him not to go. Friday night came and after an early supper John went and put on his Sunday pants.
He told Nellie not to wait up for him; he must go. On the way to the tent he told himself, if this is fake I have to tell Jessie. John went into that tent. He watched, listened, and drank in all that he saw and heard. He went back on Saturday night. Then he went again.

John began to hunger after the joy that these people had. He made up his mind however that Friday night would be his last night to go to those meetings. Friday, at work, he wrestled his thoughts on how he should not be wasting his time. Also he could not keep Nellie so upset. Sometimes God has his own thoughts about our lives. When the time came, John walked into the tent and had so many thoughts in his head it should have exploded. This service was different from the earlier ones or was he different. Instead of just hearing noise and emotion, John Kelly saw and listened with a new perspective. He felt a drawing that he could not understand. Like waves over water, the crowd began to get quiet and began to sing unto the Lord. John had never heard anything to compare to this singing. He started weeping. He raised his hands unto the sky, as many others were doing. He began to talk and cry at the same time. He experienced a joy that began to well up inside and came bursting out from his mouth. Wow! Such a closeness to God. It was something that he could not have dreamed up. He felt as if he had been taken to the presence of God in that second. He was lost into a time with God. Hours later on the way home, John wondered how do I explain all of this to Nellie.

As soon as he came into the kitchen, she was waiting up for him. She was going to tell him, that was it; no more going to those meetings. Nellie looked at John, and he was glowing when he came into the kitchen. He was so passionate when he told her of the events that he had seen and experienced. Nellie did not share this passion for this gift and experiences. John shared his story with his family and friends over the next few days. No one wanted to hear any of it. Nellie grew more concerned about what was his mental state. John was far too zealous toward things of the Lord, she told his brother.

She prayed earnestly. She felt a fear that she did not understand. Was this Bible, or was this a false doctrine? One day, Nellie, so confused, telegraphed her mother for train tickets.

That was a desperate move, as she and her Mom were not close.

Nellie and the girls were off to Parson, Kansas, for a time to gather her wits about this that John was bringing to their lives. Nellie hoped to seek understanding and most of all God's will for her family.

It was good to see her old place. The Peck house was so beautiful. Then came the thought, since her father's death, it was a house not a home. She had gotten married, her brother Willie had died, and her brother Edgar left Parson never to return. It was not a home.

Nellie wanted the girls to know of their grandmother and where she came from. Nellie's Mom bought the girls each a stack of clothes. Velma, the oldest, formed a bond to the grandmother.

Nellie's thoughts were of her husband more as each day passed. She would find herself walking all over the house. The empty rooms became her place of refuge. That's where she read the letter that John had sent to her. He was begging her to come home or send for him.

On a star light evening as she tucked the girls into bed, one of the girls asked, "When are we going home to daddy? I miss my daddy." Nellie rushed out of the room and went to the room where she was staying, and fell across the bed. After crying, prayer from deep inside of her came forth. She fell asleep and had a dream that changed her life.

The dream was Jesus, John, and her children were on the bank of a lovely river, and she was on the opposite shore. Nellie was so alone on this shore. Jesus stepped to the edge of the river, and reached out his arms toward Nellie. He motioned for her to come to the other shore. Nellie begin to step into the water's edge. She awoke with a peace that she did not know was possible.

Within a couple of days she obtained returning tickets and packed up the girls, as well as all the luggage. Nellie telegraphed John to meet them at the train station. Upon arriving, John was at the station waiting; trying to guess what she would say or do. She told him of the dream and how she crossed over. Nellie, John, and the girls went home.

In a home prayer meeting, Nellie quietly received the gift of the Holy Ghost. She found that at the other shore is where you need to be if Jesus is there. They began a life of ministry that would impact their families and many of God's children, even communities in the states of Arkansas, Kansas, Oklahoma, Iowa, and even Texas.

# 3

## Hosey Dances In Davenport

John and Nellie Kelly had grown in their life and in the Lord.  Summer of 1939, their two younger daughters, Lela and Lenora were young and still at home.

John was working and ministering as assistant pastor at the church.  Nellie had began to sew for several ladies in their community and in Davenport.

One of the church family members, Brother Hosey, had been in a terrible accident.  Hosey had been burned badly.  All of the skin, flesh, and part of the bones were gone from his right lower leg and foot.  Hosey had stayed in unbearable pain for close to three years.  The pain would vary.  The medical help back then was not much for burns of this level.  Hosey asked his church family to simply pray that his pain would become where he could handle and deal with it.  John and several other prayer warriors initiated praying for an answer to their brother's cry.

---

Their church was located in an old warehouse building down on Second Street, just two streets up from the Mississippi River. The area contained warehouses, bars, and etc.

A week or so went by of the repeated prayers and interceding for Hosey. During a prayer meeting, the Lord spoke to John. He was told to have the prayer band to begin chain fasting. Information about a specific day they would gather came later for the prayer meeting for Hosey. Pastor was in agreement with waiting to hear the time from the Lord.

The saints agreed to particpate until God said stop. They were excited to be involved in this special directive from the Lord. The church family cared for Hosey.

Sitting at the kitchen table the Lord gave John the date of the prayer meeting for Hosey. The next church service he shared this day and information with the church family. It was to be a Saturday night, that kind of shocked the church members, because that was when all the bars, would be wide open for business.

The Saturday came at the end of summer. There was expectation in the air at the church. John, Nellie, and the two daughters were there. The brothers and sisters prayed by themselves for a period of time, and then Hosey was placed on the altar. They gathered in a circle around Hosey. The children present were told to go to the prayer room or

sit on the front pews with a Bible in their hand. Lenora
went off to sleep. Lela, however, could not keep her eyes
off of the prayer group.

When the prayer began the prayer warriors were told
not to speak to each other or to Hosey until they were in the
spirit. They were to be in a respectful prayer unto the Lord.
It became loud for quite awhile. Then after about a hour
and a half the sounds took on a change. The prayer and all
sounds became very soft, with almost a gentle sound. All
those of the prayer band that remained there began to pray
the same words.

There came a bright almost blinding light. The light
hovered over the praying saints. Lela froze and she did not
move. The prayer band had began to sing a sweet song that
was not from their books, it was from Heaven. Lela noticed
the light became brighter. She heard Hosey crying out.
Then suddenly the whole prayer group moved back. Hosey
gave a loud praise unto the Lord and there was a period of a
Holy Hush.

The prayer warriors moved the circle back more.
Hosey's foot had began to grow. It grew back a brand new
complete ankle and foot. A creative miracle. Hosey jumped
up then danced. He danced and the prayer band danced. It
was pretty. He began to praise God as these believers had
not seen or heard. It was not loud, just powerful. This
night and this healing changed lives. It gave hope to many
believers and non-believers alike. The group begin to laugh,

cry, shout, and dance for joy.

Hosey danced out of the church with the prayer warrior group right behind him. He danced down toward the other end of the block and Hosey and the prayer group went into one of the wildest bars in that town.

Hosey began to pray for the bar folks. They responded and gave their hearts to the Lord. The other people in the bar seemingly did not move. In amazement the entire bar was frozen in space and in time that Saturday night. The prayer group followed suit and they would pray for people in the bar. Folks were saved and several were filled with the Holy Ghost that night. The bar shortly closed.

The local newspapers told of the news concerning Hosey's healing. Other newspapers sent out various stories of a man having a new ankle and foot. News went everywhere. The church tripled in size.

Lela never forgot that night. She passed away in 1978 after a long illness. She would speak once again about Hosey before she went into a coma and left us.

# 4

# Here I Am World

I came to bless the world on May 1, 1944. My parents were Lela and Ernest Underwood.

When I was 6 weeks old, my Mom received a telegram saying my Dad was missing in action. Then a few weeks later, the dreaded knock came at the door. My dad had been killed at the battle, called D-Day, at Normandy, France.

My grandparents took over my caregiving. At four months old, a growth was found that was causing me severe vision problems. I was legally blind. I had an operation. My grandparents fasted, prayed, and believed. There was no modern laser back then, but I got a miracle from God! I do have some vision problems, but by the grace of God with glasses I can see. That was sixty-some years ago.

I also had a respiratory related condition. I could not take the cold weather. My family was told that I needed to be in a warmer climate. My grandparents prayed for direction. By the way, I no longer have a respiratory condition.

Their oldest daughter lived in Dennison, Texas. Her husband needed help with the Sunday School ministry at his church. So my grandparents sold most of what they owned and moved to Dennison, Texas, where I could be in a warmer climate. My grandparents were in their late 50's.

Thus, Mary Jo arrived in Texas in 1945. My mom followed about a year later. I owe many thanks to my Grandma and Grandpa Kelly. They made many sacrifices for me. They did without numerous times for me to have little extras. They both really loved me and believed in me. Their gentle love, caring, and sacrifices for me meant so much. They laid down the framework for the great heritage I was given. Daily hugs, prayers, and the reading of God's Word paved a lifestyle of being real at home, as well as in church. They were role models in true sense. My heart's desire is to be real in my living for God. I use this role model phrase often, because case in point, there are so few today.

I was told repeatedly that I was a child of destiny. Today the church calls it being prophesied over. All I know is that it does work because the Bible says it will.

To know that you are believed in can help you when the world says you are nothing. It will help you know that you are worthy of God's love and His grace.

If you did not have a blessed upbringing, God will come to you with His blood and His Word. His Word will help you and deliver you. Someone will come into your life and they will show you what I am humbly trying to express. Angels can appear in odd-looking folks. It is not how many miracles we receive or how many miracles we are used in when someone else is receiving, but how much we love others that matters. God seeks out the hungry hearted.

# 5
# Dallas My Destiny

February 1952 we packed up (from Denison, Texas ) and moved to Dallas, Texas. Grandma and Pa Kelly had moved to Dallas. Momma strongly encouraged this move. My step dad had a great job offer, and her parents being there was an added sign for her. I stayed with them often off and on until I married.

When I started to school I met some new friends that would come in and out of my life (just as characters in a Charles Dickens novel). Just one I will mention at this time. There are several that has walked these last fifty years with me.

Marie and I went to school with each other and saw each other at church. Today, after 55 years, she is still one of my closest and dearest friends.

Marie Laird looked out for me at school and introduced me to other kids. They did not laugh at the skinny, cross-eyed chatterbox. I became her mouthpiece. I have been known to be someone who drags her into things and then speaks for her.

One Saturday afternoon 1954, Grandma Kelly and I went to the small local grocery store where one of the cashiers was Geneva Laird, Marie's Mom. Sister Laird went to a church that Grandma and Pa visited a lot. She was a pretty lady and full of the Holy Ghost. She was working that Saturday. Just as we were putting Grandma's items on the counter, she (Grandma) fell forward and caught herself by reaching for the counter. She was having a heart attack. Sister Laird came around the counter/check out area and came over to us. I was crying and praying. Sister Laird took Grandma and supported her from falling. She then began to pray for Grandma. In matter of minutes the Lord healed my Grandma! We praised the Lord, and other customers began praying. We paid for our groceries and hugged Sister Laird and then we left.

That same year was another time that God showed up to answer my childhood prayers. Grandpa Kelly had some time on a local radio program. Aunt Nonie sang solos on the program. She came down with a very sore throat, (this is where my answer came in to place) so bad that she could not speak the morning before the radio show. Nonie was real sick and concerned. I inquired to my Grandpa why don't I pray for Nonie, then she can sing again. Grandpa told me, I must believe and then we would pray for her to be healed. I walked over to the sofa where she was lying and we said a simple prayer of asking Jesus to heal Nonie.

The Lord healed my aunt and in just a very short time; as my Grandma (above mentioned) had been healed.

My Jesus reaches out for His children. He comes to where we are. My Grandma and Nonie were healed. He delights in healing and in blessing us. We are healed by His stripes.

Many other times in my life I did not get answers just as the two times in this short chapter. More than once the Lord had to carry me through periods of pain, sorrow, sickness, and loneliness. He would give me something in His Word to help.

While sitting at a job that had become unbearable and losing it completely, suddenly I felt others were somewhere praying for me. Knowing that there were prayers going up for me, and knowing that I was cared for calmed me down and I was able to "Carry On."

Another experience to help go on was about three to four months before my beloved Al Baby (Albert, my husband) passed away. Albert was on some medication that had to be taken at certain times and in a certain order of each other, or it could become coma or worse, for him. We had called in the refill for one of these meds and they sent it to a drugstore that closed earlier than we knew of. I spoke to the drugstore manager and he got in touch with another one of the drugstore pharmacist. They told us they would give one pill for a sum of money. We loaded up and I drove wildly to get there before the closing time. I went inside and told the pharmacist my name and who I was. He stated that he would give me a few of the pills at no charge. There just came up a lady and she was standing there beside me. She simply spoke "I know why I was to come back to this drugstore tonight, it was to pray for you!" She prayed, and those people that worked there, bowed their heads. She spoke words of comfort, and she told me things she should not have known. She left. I do not know her name, but she was an angel sent to pray for God's child in need. I got the pills, went to the car,and gave Al the medicine.

During the hard and difficult times of grieving, even now, I remember that God has given us a purpose for our existence; a reason to go on. His Word is to let us know that nowhere will we be lost in the process of this suffering. Not even death itself can threaten or change God's ultimate plan for our lives.

My perspective changes when I remember to take a glimpse of the purpose of Christ concerning me. My destiny will come to pass, be Dallas, or elsewhere.

# 6
## The Year Of Change

During my fifteenth summer while visiting my Aunt Nonie, I attended an old-fashioned outside youth revival. It was during the month of August, and it was too hot to be outside. The heat didn't seem so bad. I looked and listened at all the happenings. I noticed right away that the teens had something I did not have. I saw a joy which stirred the hunger in my soul. It was the same thing that my Grandma and Grandpa had on the inside. I wanted so much to have the same thing they had: Peace, joy, and purpose.

One of the teens was giving his testimony about finding Christ. I do not remember what all he said, but I know my heart was touched. My Grandpa got up to say something, I ran down the aisle to the old-fashioned altar. I poured my soul out to the Lord. I told Jesus I would give up anything. I did not know how, but if He showed me I would do whatever He would ask of me. Invisible heaviness left me. For me, I was born again in many aspects of my life. A few hours later in a little pond, on the out skirts of Howe, I was baptized. I was still wearing my blue silk dress and new high heel shoes.

A few weeks passed, Nonie and I were coming back from a business school class, when I became violently ill. I began to scream from the intense pain. My aunt took me to the nearest emergency room. I barely remember arriving there. I woke several days later to learn that my appendix had ruptured. I had complications after the operation. I was very ill and was to stay in the hospital for sixteen days.

The healing came slow. I had time to read and study the Bible. I read and read the Word of God. Day and night I couldn't put the Bible down. I know that my healing came from God. Time came and went. I realized that I was gaining strength. In the reading, I knew without a doubt that my life would be interesting and with a purpose. I understood the letters to the church in the Bible. They were road maps for the local church and its members.

I missed about two months of school that year. As I went back to school, I met some new Christian friends. We hung out together and even had some classes together. My friends Jerry, Joan, and David, invited me to their church. God blessed my life there. My Aunt Nonie took me to that church and she changed her membership to there also. I would attend that church for fourteen years.

Another interesting thing that happened in my life that year was my baby brother being born. My mother was 38 years old. I remember thinking how could an old woman be having a baby. I knew she would have to be in the Reader's Digest. She had a difficult time carrying the baby. A couple of days after Christmas, my Mom had to go to the hospital. Three months later, with an open C-section, my Mom gave birth to a baby boy.

Mom thought he was her miracle and Grandpa thought he was his miracle. The truth is he became a miracle for me. He was named Jonathan David after our Grandpa Kelly. He was dedicated to the Lord on Easter 1960. It was a year of change. Praise the Lord!

# 7
## What To Be Or What Not To Be...

At the age of fifteen, I began to attend a local church where I started the journey to discover my purpose in life.

The church I was attending had a small choir. I tried out for the choir, but I soon realized, a singer I was not. I came to this realization when I heard several laughing when I started to sing. I began to question the Lord, "What is my talent?"

A suggestion was made by a saint in the church that caught my attention. Their idea was to do dramas that would tell a message about the love of Jesus Christ. When I tried out for the dramas I said, "This is where I belong." I felt alive and I had found my calling.

God has purpose for our existence. We all have talents to offer the Lord. Purposes will change through the course of our life. My purpose has changed through the years. Growing and fine tuning are necessary. Sometimes it requires conquering attitudes. Other times, it requires knowing the blood of Jesus during the times that the enemy of our soul attacks us. The times we just cannot do it right. The times we tried the second and third times to do it right.

When I turned 16 years old and was attempting the fourth or fifth drama message, I played the part of a Mom with teenagers. I felt awkward and nervous. I was struggling with the part. All at once the spirit of the Lord came over me and I felt such peace. I do not recall the words of the drama. I only recall that I was adding words to my lines. I was able to relay a message with God's help that touched the hearts of people. The altar was full and many lives were touched that day.

Friendships, the feeling of belonging, and actually the first calling of ministry came from being a part of those dramas. In most of them I was even chosen to do the leading roles. Encouragement sources often came from friends, such as Jerry, who attended my church, and Jane, a teen from another church. They both believed that I would have an impact on others through the dramas.

Years later down my road of life, I was given the opportunity to write and direct drama messages/sermons. At the time, I was the Sunday School teacher for the teenagers. I became so close to the teens, it changed me and many of them became my "other children."

They felt at home at our house. We (Al and I) were so blessed by them. I still have contact with most of them. The teens in those dramas have added to my journey. The teenagers in these dramas were used of God. They have been used in different ways.

I believe the Lord can use whomever He chooses. The person needs to be willing and believe that Jesus can help them to do the things that we think are impossible. He does not just look for the most educated, the strongest, the best looking, or even the rich and famous. He sees and chooses the sincere in heart.

My Lord did not intend for me to have the talents of others, but to be me!

If you feel you do not have a calling or a talent and feel you are the odd duck of your world, know that God loves you. In every ministry God uses the odd ducks as well as the cream of the crop. You and I and other odd ducks are important. The Bible tells us that the world saw David as a young poem writer but God saw him as a future king. No matter where you are, or what you're trying to do, God is there to help you through it. God specializes in odd ducks.

# 8
## The Nerd And The Chatterbox

A chatterbox, at the ripe old age of 18 in the summer of 1962 loved the Lord, and told Him in her diary her hopes and prayers. She had an encounter with a nerd that changed her life.

The chatterbox didn't want to go to college that fall. She wanted to work in business. She loved every minute when she had attended business college. Bookkeeping (way before computers) clicked with her. Mary believed everyone had a story. At the age of six when her vision was so where she could read, it was biography, biography, biography, she chose. She began to tell folks one day I'll write a book.

Mary didn't have a boyfriend that summer, however she did have a secret crush on an older guy. He had been coming to her church, when the military would permit. He was getting out of the army soon and told the people at church, that was to be the church for him. One problem, he was engaged, with the wedding planned for a month or two away. He was an army man, but a nerd.

Albert, the nerd, was twenty-three years old. He had been a believer since his senior year in high school. He had no exposure to church in his upbringing years. He was smart. Al was tall, thin, and wore black rim glasses. If you looked (except when he was in uniform) in the left pocket there would be two to three ball point pens. His Mom and Stepdad moved during his senior year forcing him to change high schools and to lose his full scholarship. Al then chose to join the Army National Guard directly upon high school graduation.

His favorite conversations were about science inventions and how to solve crimes. Al loved working and figuring out old unsolved crimes.

Summer of 1962 he came back to Dallas to return to his work. He found that he enjoyed the little church where Miss Chatterbox went. This is where they came to know one another.

August 1962 the last night of youth camp, the teens were discussing their futures. Albert showed up and announced to the youth that he had broke off his engagement. Miss Chatterbox got excited. Another girl went over to Al and he sat down beside her to join in on the marshmallow roasting.

Then came the Labor Day weekend teen and young adult retreat. Saturday night's cookout was great. The sky was breathtaking. Stars were twinkling and suddenly a magical thing happened. A giant shooting star passed through the heavens and the group got completely silent. The youth remained that way for a short period of time. In a short time, all went back to their roasting wieners, talking, and etc. Mary looked around her. She was in a circle of young people that were near. Mary turned her head around to see who was in the circle, she saw a dear friend on one side of her and Al was on the other side. The three of them started a conversation. She had no idea what Al talked about, he talked on science. He bored those near by, except Miss Chatterbox. She was impressed with his conversation and with him.

The retreat ended. Mary decided to put a fleece before the Lord. She figured she wanted to be married within a few years. Mary asked that if possible her future prince would be one the following: **A.** The friend from church **B.** Al Baby **C.** Some wonderful guy she had not yet met.

Then the second part of the fleece was: **A.** Something would happen on Nov. 3, 1962 (why then I do not remember) **B.** The right guy would say kind and nice words or a sentence about her eyes (since she has forever believed they were so ugly).

The stupendous November third came. The Dallas area churches had planned and was having a hobo tacky party for teens and young adults. Mary had her aunt to take her. She was not missing whatever God had in store. Arriving at the fellowship hall, she went over to her friends and began to ramble on. Mary set a record for her title Ms. Chatterbox. After a bit she went over to her close friend, Edith. They sat at a table near the end. It was empty at one end. Before the stew and the other items were served to that table, the guy friend from her church came to their table. He sat down right beside her. From the end of the table a voice called out Mary. She looked up and it was Albert. Within a few minutes, he asked her to be his partner in the games and such for the evening.

Somewhere in the games, Al turned and made direct eye contact with Mary and he said to her as he had unraveled one of his mysteries, "What beautiful blue eyes you have, I could get lost looking in them." From that evening and for forty-four more years, her special name would be Blue Eyes. Quickly Mary told her friend, Edith, "He's going to fall in love with me before he knows what has hit him." At the closing of the party, Al asked could he take her home. She told him no. Mary wigged out, then left with her aunt.

The next morning at church Al sat down by her. Mary nearly passed out. He asked to take her home. That went along uneventful. After church, arriving at her home, he asked to take her out for a real date and dinner. There was a professional TV gospel group holding a concert, coming the next Saturday. She giggled and said yes. Tuesday night Albert showed up at her house. Wednesday night he came to take her to church. Directly as the services was over, he took her to a local hamburger spot. In the midst of her chocolate malt, he up and kissed her. It was a real kiss like on TV. He blurted out, "I need to talk to you. Oh, I'll just tell you, I am falling for you." "My Mom will kill you," was her reply. He started the car and drove her home. Pulling up in front of the house he gave her another real kiss! Thursday and Friday, he came by and called each day that week two to four times daily.

Then the big Saturday (11/10/1962) dinner and concert time came. That night they lived a storybook evening. She had spent a week's paycheck on a royal blue dress, gold hat, shoes, and purse. She went to the beauty shop and got her hair fixed.

Al and Mary saw at the concert numerous friends they knew, however they could only remember seeing each other's eyes. To this day, 46 years later, I cannot forget that night. At the intermission, they decided to leave. He got lost on the highway. It was not a put on. He got lost everywhere over the years. That night they stopped where there were lights to read the signs and soft drinks could be gotten. He hugged her and they kissed. Al told Mary he loved her. He shared with her the emotions he felt. Albert asked her to marry him.

The exact answer given back was, "I guess I could marry you. But you have to get my Grandpa, my Momma, and our Pastor's blessing first."

Quietly he drove off without her cold drink. She did not get to drink her malt, and now no soda. After driving awhile, they saw a sign. It read Houston, so many miles off. "Do you want to go to Houston and get married?" "No, it is past my curfew and I need to be home." Al did a u-turn on the highway and headed back for the Dallas area.

Upon arriving at her home, they both went into the living room. Her Mom was up and did not look happy. Al spoke to her mom, "Lela, uh- Sister Gentry, Mary Jo wanted permission to be engaged." The thoughts of panic hit Mary. Lela's comment was, "You can get engaged, but you cannot get married!" He was given a cup of coffee and taken to the front door.

Thus the engagement of the Nerd and the Chatterbox began. Do not laugh this really happened. It was mine and Al Baby's story. As you have figured out, we had a whirl-wind romance.

Our sons, growing up at our house, knew this was all true. Our grandchildren have trouble believing the only places we dated were church, my house, and church func-tions. Oh! We did go wild and go out to eating establish-ments.

P.S. For those who might wonder, yes, Al got the Grandpa, and the Pastor's blessing. It was ordained for the Chatter-box and the Nerd to be together.

# 9
## Esther The Quiet Ministry

One year Albert and I were struggling financially. He had been out of a job for months. We were in need of $150.00 to pay the utilities and to buy groceries. Albert, myself, and our two sons were in the back room praying that God would send us a miracle for our needs. While we were praying, we heard a knock at our front door. When we opened the door, there stood Rev. Donald Lee with sacks of groceries in his arms. He stated that the Lord had spoken to him to give us a love offering. Jesus is there when our lives are shipwrecked. He hears our prayers, knows our needs, and sends us help at the time of our need.

Rev. Donald Lee was a minister of God. He had served the body of Christ as a pastor and associate pastor. He was married to a dear friend of mine named Esther. They were married for over 35 years before God called him home. God did not choose for them to have a perfect life. They have lived out real life issues. During the years that I

have known Esther, she has endured pain, loss, disappoint-
ments as well as miracles of answered prayers for herself
and others. I have seen the Lord keep her in the palm of
His hand. The strength and peace of Jesus, as well as each
other, and family brought her through these difficult times.

Donald Lee had rheumatoid arthritis. He suffered
high levels of pain. They lost a successful home building
business, their home, and furniture. He still ministered
and Esther still served others. Esther stayed steadfast
although she went through some scary times. Her family,
also her church family carried her. Donald Lee was attacked
with cancer. God healed him. They continued in ministry.
Sickness attacked him again. This time Esther's life changed
when Donald Lee was called home to be with the Lord.
Esther's ministry however did not go on vacation. It blos-
somed.

Esther's ministry is powerful, while it is ever so gentle and always behind the scenes. She helps and she serves
others. She is everyones Aunt Esther or sister. She has
been at the hospital when needed, helped with weddings,
made picture books, cooked and cleaned, and most of all
been a prayer warrior. During her best times she did not
take the credit. She would insist on staying behind the
scenes while others received the applause. I cannot count
the occasions where we shared a church project and I
received the applause and thanks.

Esther's ministry is real, but she chooses not to have

any limelight or applause. There should be a honor hung for her in the Christian Hall of Fame.

At one time in Esther's life she suffered from migraine headaches. She was at a restaurant waiting to be seated. Her head was hurting so much she could hardly stand there. A man walked up to her and asked if he could pray for her. He prayed for her there in the restaurant. Her party was seated at a table and by the time they were seated her headache was gone. She tried to find the man to thank him for praying but he was nowhere in the restaurant.

She believed the Lord sent an angel to pray for her. To this day (over 20 years) she does not suffer with headaches anymore.

God has used Esther's quite ministry, to help, encourage, and change lives for the better. So if you do not have an Aunt Esther or Sister Esther in your life, please know that God became flesh and He shared the human body conditions, hurting, pain, loneliness, being laughed at, not belonging, as well as others deserting you and even denying they knew you. Jesus, the Great I Am, cares for the one who is hurting. His attention is to the times of the heart breaking in two.

That does not mean our problems or unbearable issues go away, but that He is there with you. He will restore what the devil has stolen.

# 10
## The Entangled Lamb

David, my brother, arrived March 1960. He is the namesake of our precious grandfather, who inspired us both to serve the Lord.

Born fair and multi-talented, the Lord used David from his birth to bring joy to others. It was very soon clear that he was given a gift of talking and speaking.

When he was three to six years old, he had a play jeep and he loved it. He followed Grandpa Kelley around listening to the hope and destiny we have in Christ Jesus. David being fifteen years younger than I, became an uncle by the age of four.

In younger years, he drew others to where he was. People listened to what he was saying. He did well in school. He would get excited about learning and social interaction. He enjoyed a strong liking in playing the guitar.

David was (and is) so creative and talented. He came up with the most fun things that gave his nephews many good memories and quite a few times to laugh at their parents.

Around the time David entered his teens, our Mother had an operation that went wrong. The operation caused other operations to follow. Numerous medicines with the illness and pain changed hers and David's life.

Upon turning fourteen years old, David began to work just to help out and to be busy. Being smart, the love for learning remained. In high school his grades dropped and his absences increased. David was forced by life to deal with things far beyond his years without a lot of outside emotional support.

When someone in a family is going through an illness or trauma, it can be forgotten that the spouse and children are attacked also. They tend to be forgotten during those times. The loneliness of that can be horrific.

The church they attended was small and did not have many teens. David played the guitar there. Teens want to have other teen friends.

David turned to friends at school, as others teens did and do. He started to go out to places with the kids that had befriended him. He was trying to find his way and place in life.

David's friends thought he was cool. Being cool was important at that age. He enjoyed the parties and fitting in. Then there came a time that it was different.

David soon realized that his friends and choices did not bring so much happiness anymore. It all soon formed as an entanglement to him. He would take care of his rabbits or ride his motorcycle. He played his guitar and went time and again with friends, however there was still the empty feeling.

He would experience great loneliness, and often a heaviness. David had a hole in his heart that only Jesus can fill. Jesus can take away the entanglements of life.

Big sister lived in Dallas and came on weekends. That was not enough help. Many family members cared and checked on them, but that was a difficult road to walk down so young.

We asked Momma to come with David, or let him come to live with us. She could not do that. We understood that home and life there gave her a sense that she was, and would be, okay.

David didn't have many normal days. He had no time to just be a teen. He worked long hours, tried to keep a house, and cared for Mom. He was forced to quit school. David did an adult's role of trying to hold a family and home together. David made a difference, even though he was not aware that he did.

January 11, 1978, Momma passed away. After the funeral services, David came for a short time to be with us.

David wanted some time to be by himself to sort life out.

A few weeks later I talked to my pastor. I asked for agreement in prayer over David. I requested the same from some of our close friends from our church. They joined in and thus the prayer began. David does not know that Al and I, from the day we were engaged, prayed together but the oneness of prayer started then and continued on stronger and stronger.

Between the two of us, Albert was the first that had an assurance. Albert told me that David would not only find peace, but that he would marry a Godly girl. Then he told me that David would be used to help many others. That is true, including some help to his sister and nephews years ago, and during these many years that have passed.

August 1978, a minister came to our church that had never been there or never came again. He walked towards me. I was standing at the end of the pew. He spoke a confirmation about David and his future. Thoughts and feelings let me know that a phone call would be the beginning of a change for David.

What phone call, I knew not where or when. Months followed, then one unforgettable night at 2:20 a.m. the phone rang and I answered it as I grabbed my Bible. I grab my Bible when I get late telephone calls. It was David on the line.

He spoke of being in an apartment, and he wanted help. David was in desperate need. All of us have been desperate or will be at some point in our lives. He knew that Jesus was the answer.

The love of God came into that apartment at once for David. That kind of love is always more real and more powerful than anything that our lives could be hit with. It wasn't words or deeds that brought peace or help. It was great love that came to him when he was in need of it. That "love beyond words" was sent to David that night. It shook that apartment! It was the divine unconditional love of the Good Shepherd.

Later in another chapter, I will share how he married the godly, steadfast, and beautiful girl Elaine. Her walk with God and everyday life is a miracle.

About a year later, he received the Holy Ghost and received such a love for others. Did his life no longer have problems or mistakes? No, again I say no! The devil does not give up on one who God chooses to make a difference. David's life has continued to show the awesome power of the Blood of Jesus.

Time came quickly. The Lord began to tug at David about ministering and preaching. David would give the Lord good arguments. The Lord, praise His name ,won the arguments.

David started to preach and minister. His ministry and callings are not run of the mill. God knows what the body of Christ needs.

David speaks in a manner to where others can laugh, and cry. Either way, people relate to what God desires to speak to them. He connects with others. He has a special calling for the ministry of altar calls, letting us know the Lord is there knocking and wanting us to let Him in.

Please remember the Lord's love for the entangled times of life!

# 11
## The Elevator Prayer

An urgent moving prayer, entitled "Elevator Prayer" began for me in 1972.

I was working for a large corporation at the new general office building. My department was on the fourth floor. Often, work would dictate to go to other floors.

On a routine work day, I got into an elevator with a young man. I did not care for elevators, however I could deal with them. We had went down a couple of floors and the elevator stopped. The doors did not open!

I waited, but the doors remained closed. The man was tense. After some time passed, I got uneasy and started to pray. The gentleman moved away from me. He moved against the elevator wall. I prayed more earnestly. I started praying from Genesis to Revelation. I began to say, "Lord you kept the three Hebrew children from the fire." About a hour later I had finished quoting the Old Testament. I would bellow out, "You used Moses to bring the children of Israel out of Egypt."

Then I started on New Testament with Mighty God, that you are, you walked on the water and calmed the storm. You heard a spiritually hungry Roman Centurion praying and etc. The affirmations went on for quite a long period of time. I was building my faith for myself.

Then after faith had clicked in, I spoke in the Name of Jesus, "Doors now open!!" Then I uttered, "One and True God, in the name of Jesus, door open." The elevators doors opened at once. The young man nearly knocked me down getting out of that elevator. I believe he'll also never forget that elevator ride.

From that time on, when things or people have urgent needs, I pray the elevator prayer. Speaking the word of God will open whatever door has us or our loved ones trapped by.

# 12
## Don't Get Excited

Family together times were interesting with our family.

Summer 1977, Albert, the boys, mom, David, and myself camped out. There we all were on lovely Lake Texoma. We pitched two large tents. Momma and Al fished. The boys were in and out of the water's edge. The first day and night came and went with out much ado. The second night was approaching. Tim started breaking out, itching, and was miserable. David and Steve collaborated and got a great idea – let's have a bond fire and roast marshmallows. They gathered up sticks and brush. They went on additional stick searches. I wanted to be of a help and so I poured lantern fluid on the present stack of wood. I poured a little more oil on, so I would be sure of a good job. David and Steve returned with a large bunch of twigs and short pieces of wood. Being the organized one in the group, I went into one of the tents to obtain the marshmallows. Returning with marshmallows in hand, my eyes watched David pouring lantern fluid onto the stack of wood. Walking towards them, it was twilight changing to darkness. David finished off the can of oil he had upon the wood. Suddenly, for no apparent reason, the stack of wood which had a small fire started, turned into a loud noise. The noise was accompanied with a blaze of 8 to 10 feet high. Flames were flickering and then a second loud boom occured. The whole area of that beach turned daylight. The lake guard, firemen, and many other folks showed up!

We had a lot of explaining to do that evening. People asked questions over and over. Tim told them I had put some oil on the wood. After just a few hours, the visitors left. Believe it or not, no tickets were given to us. We settled down and roasted the marshmallows.

Together, David and I let out with anything but soft laugher. We told Momma and Al Baby the details of the oil. Al Baby was not quite happy with us on this one.

I believe this was one of the last camping trips we went on.

Another famous camping trip was on the same lake. Yes, for real!

It was a trip where the fishing didn't go well for Albert. He got bored. The boys and Mom were swimming or playing in the water. Al was an inventor. He had several good inventions that we all were proud of, however there were some inventions only he saw the true value of. Albert's creative juices began to flow. He stirred around and some way he had rigged up materials. He spent hours of hard work. The end results being – he built a raft! Al got the raft out onto the water. Then he climbed aboard. I and the rest were looking on. The raft went out some distance. Mom and I needed to start something to eat and returned towards the campsite.

Others were all laughing as they waved at Albert. Al enjoyed the raft until it started to sink. Al was standing in the middle of the raft saluting to all onlookers. He stood at attention and remained in the center of the raft. It soon was totally underwater. He got up and out of the water.

We were informed, as he stepped on to the beach to where we all were, "That a captain stays with his ship."

Rounds of hugs were given to Al Baby, the captain. A good time was had by all.

The spring of 1981, I was a library clerk for the school district. The school library was near the end wing of the building, near a street entrance.

Stephen had been driving a year or so. His VW bug was not working right so he borrowed my Dodge Charger. He and David were to take Tim to school, then run some errands.

Midmorning I went into the school hallway walking towards the main office. I looked up and there was David, and Steve was directly behind him. Together, and at the same time they both yelled out, "Don't get excited!"

I knew without any other communication that they had killed Tim and wrecked my car. They had only totaled the car.

# 13
## Elaine The Bug Catcher

At the time Elaine caught this bug she was a high school student. She was one of the most outstanding youths I ever taught.

She had started to date a young man which was a fellow student at her school. This is a kicker, he claimed he didn't believe in God. She discussed with him more than one time how real the Lord was.

Now to our short story on bug catching. On a cold Sunday in February, something interesting took place. My sons and I went out to get into our car to go to church. It was gone. It had been taken, stolen from our drive way! Albert's VW bug that he loved so. He was working that weekend out of town. We went back inside. I called him. He had me to call the police.

I was told, from the police, that VW bugs were fun

and popular so to forget it and call our insurance. I telephoned the church and explained our dilemma. I got the boys to get down and we prayed that the bug would show up before their dad came home.

Later, that same afternoon, a car drove up. It was Elaine and the young man I had heard about. She told me that they had been driving and she thought they had found Albert's bug. They drove me over to where the VW was, about one or two miles from the house. Some folks had been making circles in the snow and ice with the bug, and the engine was jammed. The engine was frozen is what the officer said. I forgot to mention that I got so excited when I saw the bug that I jumped out of his car and fell on the sidewalk. Elaine helped me up. The bug was towed home. When Al baby came home there it was. The next week it was fixed.

Elaine, the bug catcher, has helped and assisted the Lord in many areas of my life and my family. Her prayer life, faithfulness, and quiet elegance is admired. The Lord sends to our lives some special people to help us. It can be to find a VW and other things, as to add to our lives.

She is one of the best friends to me. Elaine is endearingly caring. She is my favorite sister-in-law. Really she is my sister-in-love.

# 14
## Intense Fellowship

My Al Baby (my nickname for Albert, my treasured husband for 44 years and 10 days) and I became friends and prayer partners. Please note the word, became!

When we first married, we realized early that we were from and lived in different worlds. Our personalities also were as opposite as any two people could have.

So if your marriage is not in the Happy Ever After Stage, or you do not believe it can ever be, let me share some things that brought serious and very intense fellowship to us.

We argued over style of raising our children. Our children had to endure this. We argued about money and debts. These I understand are common problems.

The last and the really stupid thing we fought over

many years and caused hurt was getting lost. Yes, I stated, getting lost. Albert had a real problem with losing directions. He had the highest grade average score in high school and made the deans' list in college, but he got lost everywhere.

I'm a nut on not varying from a certain step by step way to or from anywhere. This brought unbelievable hurtful discussions.

During the years of 1976 to 1989, he worked a part time job. He had two jobs, so his body was pushed. This did not help a family in their everyday life struggles.

After thirty years, in 1992, I had a serious back operation. It was a long ordeal something began to transpire.

I began to see Albert as the Lord saw him. He quit blaming me for all of our problems. I heard Al Baby many times, but I did not understand that I was to listen. In our marriage, we loved each other like few couples know to love; however, it took a lifetime to learn how to be best friends.

This little page/chapter was such a personal one. So for those that think or feel your marriage is not right or worth much, or even that it will never get any better, wrong!!

Quit trying to remake your mate and request your vision of them to be changed. Ask the Lord to help see them as Christ sees them. It is not easy, but Christ will bring it to a reality. Stop comparing them to other people. Quit right now comparing spouses.

Learn their strengths, and laugh together; a must! Tell them what you like about them, not what you do not like.

I know that praying for each other to be changed did not work. My Jesus did what Al Baby and I could not do.

# 15
## The Boys

In our large city, there is a famous sports team called "The Boys". However the boys in this chapter would be my two sons.

Now being grown men, they look so much alike it is uncanny. A case in point: A couple of years ago both Steve and Tim with their wives went to the same hairdresser (for haircuts). She is a dear family friend and Tim and Liz went in to get their haircuts on a Thursday evening. The following Saturday Steve and Karen came in and got hair cuts. A few days later one of the other hairdressers approached Jeanie. She asked, "Don't you go to church with Mary Jo and her family?" Jeanie's reply was, "Yes, why?" The other operator hem hawed around, then she blurted out, "Mary Jo seems to be a good church-going woman. Her son seems to be nice, but Thursday he brought one wife in and then Saturday he brought in different wife. What kind of church do you all go to?" Jeanie explained that they were brothers. Both gave out with such laughter. The beauty shop rang with laughter.

Onward and upward, the boys are each their own person and different men. They have one wonderful quality. They want to please and help people. They give to others of themselves. They have gifts that, as a mother, I stand back and look in awe of.

The oldest (the firstborn) son was named long before he was born. Albert and I were talking about how many children we would have someday. Al said, "Our first child will be a boy and I want him named Stephen!" He wanted a house full of sons to carry on the Brinkley name. He was named Stephen.

Steve, as a young child, was loving and wanted to please those around him. We hugged often and he would say, "I wove you." He always stayed close to one of us. I loved that wherever I was I knew he was right there. Steve had strong interest in building, inspecting, and taking apart something, anything. He was also given a voice. The Kelley music talents did go on in some of us.

Al Baby and I hugged lots more than once daily. I wanted this loving child to share in this tradition. I started a routine with Steve of hugging him, attempting to sing to him, and telling him Bible stories. His first months, when he did not want to sleep at night, I would rock him and pray over him. Needing and giving love, the Word of God and music was placed into him. Some by genetics, some by parents, and most of all by our God.

He began with totally unprepared parents. That is an understatement! I was over protective, and his dad, Al Baby, a perfectionist. Steve checked to see that one of us was close. He had a habit of bringing home stray dogs. Where he came up with them is still a mystery. My Mom bought him one and it had to be given away along with the others. His eyes puffed up and he broke out. He had allergies. One of the Brinkley gifts. Steve sat and played for hours with wooden toys that connect together.

By the time he started off to Kindergarten, he could read and do math. Building erector sets was commonplace for him. When he could create or please others, he had that special look of "I am the man, mommy." He would take apart household electronics. Those days brought interesting conversation when dad came home. Then they laughed and decided how they could make this a better product and help the human race.

In his teen years, he sang in a church youth musical group, along with his school choirs and a special singing group. Oh yeah, he seemed to have a real love for one of those computer machines. These things, as well as girls and his souped up VW bug, gave him pride and purpose. He and his best friends, sure liked to drive up and down a street that all cool high school students just happened to be on Friday nights.

He graduated with honors and went off to a Bible college in south Texas. He met new friends. One was a girl named Karen. The next summer they got married.

Twenty-five years later, he and Karen are now grand-parents of Miss Emma Grace. Today Steve is known for helping others. He loves and serves the Lord. As Mom and Dad knew he would.

Steve and Karen have two sons. The oldest is Luke, and their younger son is Matthew. Both boys love cars. They also know to call 1-800-dad.

Stephen has had challenges that Mom and Dad did not ever plan on. He has worked 80 to 110 hour weeks for years.

Steve has went through colon cancer and was healed by the Grace of our Lord Jesus, in addition with the help of his Dad, family, and ours pastors, Brother and Sister Davis. The Lord has developed a man of God, and one that shows some of his Mom's emotional side. I think that some days he understands his mom.

Stephen's name means "a crown" and fits the first born.

The youngest, our baby son Timothy, as a very young child was outgoing, bubbly, never met a stranger, and was always talking and telling them his life story. He loved life

Tim was in the hospital numerous times.  He got scared of white jackets.  Despite all this he stayed happy and never still.  He laughed and wanted to pray with you.  He was a positive child.  Colored blind as can be, he wanted to wear unusual pieces of clothing together.

He became more ill and then had one severe sickness as he was turning four years old.  On a night in late spring, Tim was in the hospital.  I was praying for him to get better.  Nothing different than other times and other prayers.  Tim's fever broke suddenly.  He sat up and he wanted a jelly donut.  In a couple of days we brought him home.

Instead of several health and learning issues that the doctors tried to prepare us for, God had his own plans for Timothy's future.

I forgot to tell you that are reading this that when I was pregnant, about three months along,  I started bleeding heavy and fell in the bathroom at work.  I reminded God and myself of what the doctors told me.  I would never be able to get pregnant again but I was.

The Lord spoke.  The words of comfort to me were, "This son will tell of Me in business places where you do not go. He shall speak of Me to businessmen. I shall be His God. He will stand in difficult times. I will place in him gifts, that men will know more of Me."

An hour or so later I was taken to the hospital. The first doctor told me I would lose the baby. Soon Al and our pastor (the one who married us) came into the hospital room. They prayed and pastor spoke, "You will not lose this child. He will be born on June 4." Guess what day Tim was born on? You're right, June 4.

Tim's neatest gift began at a young age when he was called to be a peacemaker. He has goodness, honesty, and love for others.

Back to when Timothy had been touched after a simple prayer. He did not have pneumonia again. At the age of four he could read and he could do math. His favorite thing to do was talk and more talk. He loved to read the Bible books and play board games. Tim enjoyed sports watching and playing sports. He played soccer for four years. Tim shared his day and wanted to pray with you.

During the middle school and high school years, Tim won math contests. Tim was in the newspaper and on Television for excelling in academics. Tim, in his teens, took an active interest in church activities and was really good in the youth dramas. He showed his caring for others and the Lord in the characters he played.

In college he had a penpal from one of the church missionary families. They actually met each other when she came to our house for a holiday visit. Two years later he went to see her on a few trips. They wrote, telephoned, and soon fell in love. They were married the summer of 1988.

Twenty years later, Tim and Liz are blessed with two children, Michael and Aimee. Tim has learned to lean on his God for so many facets of life. Tim's wife, Liz, has been ill for a few years, and he has had some real health issues himself. Tim is an overcomer by the blood of the Lamb.

Timothy's name means "an honor to God" and that name fits him.

### To The Boys

Thank you dear sons for putting up with us as parents. Thank you for becoming men of God, which was mine and your Dad's heart's desire.

# 16
## He Won't Drown

When Steve was four years old, Al and I took him to an amusement park. Albert and Steve rode numerous rides. They ate junk food and then would ride more rides. Steve was not use to that. He was not use to being out in the hot sun for long periods of time. The rides with the up and down and whirling around, the heat, and the foods started to take their toll. Late that afternoon, he got so tired. Steve pleaded to go home. Albert told him, "Son we will after the ride we are in line for and then we will take you home." Albert gave him a hug.

The line moved forward. We were at the area where you are placed into the car of the ride. I had never seen a ride quite like this one. The car looked like a log. The young attendant said something about plumes. I then did a double take upon seeing the water. It surely was deep.

At that moment in time, and suddenly before I could prevent him, Steve fell or jumped into the water. I cried out, "He won't drown! The Lord will help me save him." I dove in the deep water. Of course, I did not know how to swim but did that matter? I landed hard! Then I realized that the water was shallow not deep. My body was experiencing pain everywhere. The water was only two or three feet deep. I was thinking I would be joining loved ones on the other shore.

Steve was standing up laughing. Al and the young ride attendant pulled me out. I could not stand for a long while. Steve tried to reassure us that he was having fun. He became upset as his Daddy had to get me to the car. The entire crowd around us laughed. On the trip home Albert and Steve laughed, repeating my Alamo cry of "He won't drown". Several days went by before the bruises and pain were any less.

The Lord was with me, as He has been so many times since. I tend to dive into things.

When I reflect and think of that day, it brings loads of laughter. It brings back treasured memories.

# 17
## The Rock And The Heart

Several years ago, I asked my sons how they would explain their Mom and Dad and their home life.

One of them told me that Dad was like a rock. He was solid and you knew he would always be there. Mom you were the heart, believing in us. Your love, laughter, and faith coming mostly from inside. Wow that sounds good doesn't it?

Albert was such a gift of solidness and was there for all of us. He believed in me, except my driving which I'll talk about later. He dealt with me growing up with our boys. He encouraged me in every area of faith and the many things I attempted to do for our Lord. When I went to work he told me I'd become good at whatever my niche was. He, over the years, was the president of my fan club.

Al didn't like painting inside or outside of a house.

One year I decided that our house could be painted by the boys and myself. I put Tim on the bottom, me in the middle, and Steve on a ladder. Not only did we paint the house, but also the porch, and a lot of the front yard.

During the painting, I remember Tim asking me to quit slapping him with paint! We laughed a lot during this project.

My eyes used to be crossed and plagued with other issues. I was ashamed of my eyes. Al loved to look right into my eyes. He made me feel they were lovely, plus he would tell me that my eyes were beautiful.

We held hands most of the time, even more so as we got older. I loved to dress up for him for every day times, just have an Al Baby night, or go for a hamburger. I always placed my hand on his knee, while he drove or while sitting in church. When we looked at each other even the world stood still while folding clothes.

I am going to share a couple of moments that happened during our 40 years.

First let me make a side comment that a friend said to Albert and myself, "You two are too close." Maybe she was right. Why would I agree and say that statement could be right? Because now that he is gone missing him is a part of every area of my existence.

Back to describing Brinkley moments, the good stuff of Al Baby and me at home. I could tell you of the many love notes and how we would hug whenever one of us left or entered the other's presence. Love notes were left on a pillow, in the ice box, and even in a peanut butter sandwich.

Happy and romantic times would entail of watching old movies while eating loads of ice cream. During these numerous special evenings, we'd begin to declare of our love for each other. Often, as some years came and went, there would be added dream talking of our retirement years together.

Some things he did not encourage real well. One of those things being me teaching myself to drive. One night when Al was working, I put Steve in the car and had him to hold a Bible as I drove. I hit a couple of trees. No real problems. I simply told Albert how the trees just seem to hit us. Another driving time, I had went to the drug store. When I started to return home I was complaining to Steve about how it was so dark that I could not see. Steve told me if I would turn the car lights on, it would help us Momma. As I turned on the lights, suddenly I realized I had driven onto the street median. At once I drove off the median with a jolt, and we went home. Albert still wanted to drive all the time even years later.

When I first got married, I only knew how to prepare four meals. I was rotating the four meals, but Albert still complained. I decided to put pink, blue, and green food

coloring in all the foods to change them up. The pink bis-
cuits were okay but he refused to eat the green mashed
potatoes! I cried and Albert helped start my collection of
school and church cookbooks.

Now I am going to tell you a little secret about us.
In our old house, going from the small bedroom into the
den, there was a step. One of our special things was that I
would stand on the step and he would stand in the den, and
we would kiss!

Back to me being the heart; I love people and that is
where being the heart comes in.

We weren't always perfect, but I like to believe that
the carpenter took pieces of wood and developed them over
the years into the rock and the heart.

Your family will be a piece of cake to work on after us!

# 18
## The On-Time God Supplies

Spring of 1973, the flowers were in full bloom. We had only one little problem, a financial crisis.

Albert had been laid off for months. We had prayed and prayed. I did not understand the depression and pressures he felt! I knew what I was feeling and let him know it. Today that haunts me deeply. I was not as supportive as I like everyone to believe. I was young, and I thought far too much about me on this subject.

Our God is on time when we go through trials. Some of them are answered on His time! We want God's will to be done and completed ASAP when we are hurting.

Three specific times during the last few months before he got another job (the first was one for urgent survival) God showed up and showed out to supply our family's needs.

Summer brought us hot Texas days and nights. We became desperate on money issues. There arose the time that required us to have $150.00 to pay the water and gas bills. We were down to hot dogs, popcorn, and very few potatoes left. Remembering these events gives me strength today. Albert and I gathered Steve and Timmy to the old den. It was a serious time in our lives. We all knelt, joined hands, and prayed together I knew the answer was beyond what I knew or could figure out. We had not told anyone of the amount or about needing more food.

The Brinkley prayer meeting was over, and we felt no great faith at that point. There was a knock on the old den door. Brother Donald Lee entered in. He had brought a pounding, for you younger ones, that means gifts of food, items, and money. He showed up with the amount of $150.00 and sacks of food and some personal items.

Weeks later the following two miracles happened as well. Albert and I prayed together with the boys. They had left the room and he held me gently. There was a silence which was always a miracle in our household. He held me as only he could do. At the same time, we cried out to the Lord for help.

The next day or so he needed to do something to keep busy. Al had a garage full of boxes to clear out. You all should know I was a neat freak, and he was an extreme pack rat. The garage was full of boxes. He picked out just a few boxes by random and brought them into the old den.

After hours of cleaning and throwing out old papers he stopped. Albert came over and kissed me with a powerful kiss and laughter. Al had found a real old insurance check for a couple of months of what his salary would have been. He was able to take the check downtown to the insurance company office. They gave him a new check for the amount. The Brinkley's went to a local steak house and celebrated that night. We shared the news at our church to encourage others.

Now the third miracle during a year of jobless trials was this: On one of the last hot Sundays in the afternoon, I got a phone call. The voice was muffled. Words were spoken to me, "Go to your mailbox." Per instructions I went to the mailbox. I found a gold envelope with the scripture about your need being supplied on it. Enclosed in that gold envelope were hundred dollar bills.

Albert began to believe in himself once again. The most important thing was he was able to believe that a job would open up. He had operated under fear that would grasp hold of him. Al Baby spoke and sounded like himself. He began to even look for a job again. He went to work within a month. The first job was for an AC firm. It was less than 40% of his former income, but we did not care.

Shortly after he went to work for the AC company, I was approached by a friend at my job. It seemed that her husband's company needed someone in the purchasing department, so Albert applied for that job. He received the position which lasted for years.  The salary was exactly what his former salary was.

When that company closed, he went to work for the best job (he was in his mid-forties) he ever had.  It was the one he stayed with until he went home to be with the Lord.

Our perspective changed when we caught a glimpse of Jesus in it all.

# 19
## A Promise Kept

In the summer of 1959, John and Nellie Kelly (my grandparents) had been in an intense time of fasting and prayer. Their prayers were for their daughters and their grandchildren. In 1959, of the six daughters, only one was attending church faithfully. Only that one was allowing the Lord to be Lord in her life. Their prayers included the 24 grandchildren. They placed their cries before the Lord for each of them to find Christ, or if they had known and served Him to recommit their lives.

In July, hot as North Central Texas can be during the day, Grandma and Grandpa and myself (which was a trio most of my first 18 years) was sitting on their front porch. The both of them spoke to each other about these requests to God. Grandma first shared and then Grandpa shared. They had been given separately the same answer. The answer was that each of their five daughters would be serving their Lord, and would make a difference in someone else's life before their homecoming would take place. Wow! The answer on the grandchildren got my attention. It was that 21 would serve the Lord. What is more grabbing was the last part of the answer, or at least what they both stated to me. I'd make a life-changing decision for Christ. Within four weeks I gave my heart to Jesus totally, and for my life has forever been changed.

Grandma passed away in August. It was the night after Grandpa was in a horrible car accident (13 days after I accepted the Lord).

Grandpa sat in a wheelchair for six months. Mom and my 12 year old brother took care of him until February 1973.

Grandma and Grandpa saw four of the five daughters and eight of their grandchildren become a living part of their promise.

Let me just share with you a couple of the daughter's stories.

One auntie, while she had been married to a preacher for years, heard one of her daughters sharing what God had done. Auntie ran to an old-fashioned altar. She worked with a passion for seven years helping struggling and hurting people. She had a massive heart attack one fall evening and was called home.

Another auntie, had lived through two rounds of cancer. Then years later moved into a small community in Arkansas. A new neighbor came over to welcome her. The neighbor came often. This neighbor simply happened to be on fire for God. The two got to be close friends. The auntie found out that now she had a heart condition. My Mom got a call that auntie had been praying with her neighbor. Only a couple of months later, Mom gets a call and this auntie had a marvelous renewing and full restoration with the Lord. Auntie began to share Christ with those near her, and she used a gift that had been given to her at the age of fifteen. She had a massive heart attack and went to be with the Lord. If heaven needed a piano player, I am sure she has helped them out.

Wow, and double wow!

Grandma & Pa passed away in 1972 and 1973. Now this is 36 years later. I have been blessed in the last three months to have had contact with a few cousins. I have been allowed to see, know, and now hear about nine more cousins that are living for and changing others lives for our Lord Jesus Christ. My grandparents saw a little of that 1959 promise come to pass. It will be completed very soon.

If you did not a have a Godly promise over you or you do not have a promise for your loved ones, ask for one. He is just and faithful. If God makes a promise it is a promise kept!

Acts chapter two tells us that it is for our children and their children and their children, too. So let us carry on!

# 20
## That Was My Baby

1980 was a year of importance to the Brinkley household. The oldest son, Stephen, began to drive. Within a year, he lived through a few car accidents. In most of them, he totaled the cars.

The accident I would like to share with you is when I lost it, and I do not even believe my actions.

Rolling back my mind's memory curtains, it was a Friday night. Al, myself, and others had gathered for a time of fellowship, eating, and prayer. A favorite social experience for Christians; eating, along with fellowship.

After eating, the two teenage boys, Steve and his best friend, Scott, decided that they needed to leave for other social endeavors. The evening event that they had in mind was driving up and down the local main drag. They would be waving at the other teenagers driving by. Then stopping at a hamburger place where there would be GIRLS! Steve drove his VW bug with pictures of footprints on the back of it. Well known in the little community at that time.

Soon after their departure, there came a statement that we should have a special prayer over the two boys. The group of us prayed for their safety.

Then visiting and more eating returned. A phone call came. The information stated to us was that the police were taking the boys to an emergency room. Injuries had occurred. The families were instructed to go to that hospital ER. We took off in a flurry and had anxious emotions.

Upon arriving while checking in at the counter, an ambulance crew came rushing into the area. They had Scott on a gurney. The hospital personnel started working with him. They took Scott and left the area. I could not see Steve anywhere. I inquired as I was crying, "Where is my baby?" The police officer replied, "Madam, there was no baby, only the tall blonde teen who drove the vehicle. He should be here in another ambulance." I slapped the officer on the shoulder, screaming, "That Is My Baby!"

Albert attempted to explain that Steve was our oldest son, but that Steve and his brother were her babies. They were "The Boys."

I do not believe the officer understood. I know he did not know about being a Momma.

I got so upset when Steve was not brought to the hospital after a good long time. I was given a shot, per request of my Al Baby. He placed a call to my doctor. The doctor in turn spoke with an attending doctor at the ER. I was taken to our home. My friend, Esther came along to assist in keeping me calm. In a matter of a few minutes, a school friend brought Steve home.

Stephen told us the next day that the bug brakes suddenly went out. The VW slid, rolled over, and then came to a complete stop. Scott was thrown out onto the busy street. An ambulance came and they took Scott off. They left him there. Steve looked up and his eyes froze on a large arch way sign. It read, "Scyene Cemetery." His thoughts were that he was at heaven's gate. Just then a car came close to hitting him and it stopped fast. It was a school friend. He put Steve into his car and brought him to the house. We guessed that by the time the second ambulance came Steve was gone.

# 21
## The Class Goes To The Dogs

This is just for laughs.  So take time to laugh.

Marie and I were taking computer classes that our jobs offered.  It was a beautiful and breathtaking spring evening.  I had not been focused on the class that specific evening.  My youngest son would be getting married in June. I was thinking about the wedding plans.

After class, Marie and I were walking through the visitor's parking lot.  About 4 ½ feet higher than the road, at the edge of the visitor's parking lot, was a flat ledge. It was approximately three feet wide.  The driveway was a long slant down to the sidewalk and street.

We had walked to the end of the driveway.  There came a man walking dogs.  A large dog got loose and began to come toward us.  The dog got close and I screamed. Then I jumped, and how I ever landed on that ledge top is beside me! I have never been able to figure it out.

Marie laughed and laughed. The man got his dog. He looked so scared. He left running. Marie helped me down off the ledge. Both of us walked to the car laughing.

The Lord has a sense of humor. It shows up when we need a laugh at ourselves.

Laughter is a good medicine for our spirits and our bodies.

# 22
## The Pearl

This pearl is Edith.  The Edith that I met at church when I was in high school.  At church, she would stay close to her sister, Pat.  She was shy and quiet.  Edith seemed to hunger for the things of the Lord.  She had gifts that she knew not of.  Edith and Pat were easy to become close friends with.  I could be myself when with them.

Edith shared my dream of the Lord sending us a prince charming.  During a long and blessed summer at youth camp, the last night over twenty youth received a real encounter with Jesus.  Then the summer of 1962 began to come to an end, and my prince arrived.  (That's another story)  During the courtship, she was thrilled and helped me pray for God's will.  When the Christmas wedding took place, she was my Maid of Honor.  Edith drove my car long before I could drive.  She stood as a good friend, and stands today as one of several prayer partners.  She is our oldest son Stephen's God-mother.

Through the years, she began to grow and allow her world to enlarge. In 1969, my cousin, Paul, showed up as a pleasant surprise to us.

Edith and Paul fell in love and got married several months later. This pearl shone brighter and brighter. Within a few years, Paul attended Bible college. He and Edith started to minister. They had begun a family as well. Edith stood with Paul in ministry, and it took them several locations over the years.

Years went by and their children were grown. Edith became sick. She went to the doctor. It was found that she had cancer in the female organs. She was not given a long time to live. Edith and Paul were given information of different treatments. They looked into two of the suggested treatments. Praying that they would choose the best treatment, Edith heard from the Lord a totally different one. As Edith explained it, she heard clearly of a direction concerning what and what not to do. She was only to have the hysterectomy and not to have chemo and radiation. Edith was questioned,"What if you have missed God?" She even tried to explain her chose to the doctors. She believed she had heard from the Lord.

She called me for a sounding board and for prayer. I prayed in agreement with Edith. I believed so strongly that she had heard from God. If you knew Edith the way I knew her, (at that time) you would have believed it also.

She went through months, standing on the Word of God. I love to remember the words I heard from her several months down the road. Edith declared, "I should have been dead by now. They have ran and reran tests and I am cancer free!" She started on her road to being outgoing. She became a people person.

This pearl's oyster shell opened up. Edith turned into a Pearl of the Lord's handiwork.

Somewhere, some one reading this is asking me, "Why didn't you get a miracle?" I do not know. I know this, Jesus cares what you have been through or what you are going through.

I beg you to begin to get into the scriptures until the "why" is not what must be known, but until there is assurance of HIS peace and power.

# 23
## Never Forsaken

Pat's life (a dear cousin) showed the Lord's guiding and re-directing to green pastures.

She lost her husband and she went through grieving. She found herself on rocky trails in the valley the she had to walk through. Her spirit and emotions were restored. She was sent a lovely Christian lady friend to help while others prayed.

Some years down the road she met John. They dated and the time came when they shared their faith. They fell in love and were married. They have been married for twenty some years now. About nine years ago John and Pat were doing a ministry in a far northwestern state. Pat became ill with symptons of flu and trouble with her ears. She went to the doctor and she was placed on antibiotics. Pat shortly thereafter went into a comma. The doctors gave John a negative report that Pat would not pull out of the comma. There came a time when the medical team wanted to pull the plug, as it is said on the TV. Prayers were going up everywhere. The family was told that if she came through and came out of the coma, she'd have only some of her mental and physical capabilities.

They did not know what really would happen. Her husband and children asked for a period of time before the doctors would do anything. Ladies came to sit with her and they would help read the Bible to Pat. Believers were praying all across the country. I would speak with two of her brothers and John to keep up with her status. I believed so strongly that she had something else to do.

Weeks went by and Pat came out of the coma. There was no speech, her mental skills were not up to par, and there was no real physical movement. John had been given strength to go through all of this with her. He has been through the valley of shadow of death in this also. It is easy to overlook the family and caregivers, who suffer so much jointly in the valleys.

The reading of the Bible and the prayers moved to passionate and fervent. Months went by and Pat started talking. She was placed into long and painful therapy. I do not know the exact times of each and every stage she and John went through during this period. Her son moved into that area.

She regained use of her arms, speech, and capabilities. Therapies, Bible reading, tapes, and daily prayers, John standing in the gap, and of course medical help brought her through. She would still have issues and pain. God was real and a strong presence to both of them. A few of the medical team were changed and impacted by what they saw in Pat and John's lifes. (I do not have names or details, that's for Pat's book.)

Pat was sent to hospitals and doctors. As years passed, she regained many stolen functions of her life, as time went on. She could sit and do most things.

Several years later Pat had to go through a heart operation. She endured a painful neck procedure. More daily pain and it has been for years. She began to have such a desire to walk. She prays today for relief from pain, and to walk.

Once during a prayer meeting, even though medically it is not possible, she got out of that chair (for a short time) and danced before the Lord. Pat holds on to that experience until she is able to walk all the time.

Pat is a living, recorded (yes documented), unexplained medical miracle. In that, she still suffers in extreme high levels of pain.

Pat and John received answered prayers. Their experience has stood out. Why still the pain, I do not know. Pat tells me on the phone, "I have never been forsaken."

The source of her daily journey is Jesus and His Word. He is her refuge and her fortress. We remember the key phrase is "though I walk through the valley of the shadow of death, I will fear no evil." The part to remember is the walking through. Talking about it is easier than the walking through. She holds on to that dearly.

# 24
## The Bang That Brought
## A Blessing

In 1996, one Tuesday morning, I opened the front door. I had heard a loud bang. My car was parked out front. I parked it parallel with the sidewalk. A neighbor from across the street had backed out of a driveway and had hit my car.

Al Baby went unglued. We did not really know the lady. I had to keep him from speaking his mind and talking about the issue of the car. She and I talked. She was such a nice lady. We all got the car business dealt with, and the car got fixed. She and I got to know each other on a personal level. I found out that she had lost her husband and was a real believer. She was spirit-filled.

From time to time after the bang; Eva and myself

would exchange conversations. I didn't like the idea of her not having anyone. It would be hard not having children living here, and I could not even think of what it would be like without your husband.

Around three years of being casual friends went by. Around 2000, I noticed Eva had not been out to go to work or church for several days. That evening during my prayer time, I felt I was being told, "Go and pray for Eva. She is sick." I argued with these feelings. Each evening, when I got down to pray or had anytime of prayer, the same exact phrase of thought would return. Enough beyond my "what ifs", I yielded to the directions from the Lord.

I touched my Bible, then placed olive oil on my fingers and off across the street I proceeded. Knock, knock. My thoughts were, why no answer. Leave now. The door opened about halfway. Eva was standing there. I opened the storm door. I blurted out with "The Lord told me to come over here and pray for you. Are you sick?" Eva, weak, but with intense tones answered, "Yes!" As I gazed at her, I realized how weak she was. We prayed together.

God came down in her living room. Gentle, yet you knew God had showed up. Later she shared that it had been confirmed. God had given her a specific and definite healing. Jesus did a work for a sister needing Him to touch her body. We have become close friends. In about 2003, we started to meet periodically for times of praying together.

Al Baby went to be with the Lord. Eva has listened to my repeated conversation concerning how do I make it. I simply do not know how to live without him. I never been alone. What was God thinking?

So many ways God has used this friendship to be a blessing to us both.

Once we were talking, in her driveway, and the Lord spoke into my thoughts, "Pray now for a woman in a long black car." We started praying in the spirit, and at that minute a very long black chauffer-driven car pulled up and stopped. An apparently well-to-do woman got out and came over to us. She asked, "Are you two ladies praying for me?" "Yes", I quietly answered to her. She told us that she was from another country. She had come to this country, and then to this area to see lost grandchildren. She found out they lived a street over from us. She, in prayer, was told that she would find two ladies praying, and that she would see the grandchildren. We prayed for her, her daughter, and her grandchildren. She hugged us, told us her name, (which I ca not remember) and got back into the car and left. The grandchildren came by sometime after that, and introduced themselves to me. They knew I was one of the praying ladies. Wow!

Eva has called numerous times in the last year or so with words directly from the Lord confirming or warning about private things I was praying for. A special friend has come from that car bang.

We will all have pain of loss in our lives. Some have wonderful people or things that move in and help with that pain, and some do not. Some deal with loss, loneliness, and financial storms. They are frozen by loss. Those six hours on the Cross, Jesus knew loss.

God uses many things to bless you when you are hit by loss.

This bang became a blessing!

# 25
## The Wounded Children

The Body of Christ is made up of his dear children. As any family, the children are not perfect.

If the children are loved and accepted, when they become wounded or slip they will find their way. All know what it is to feel hurt. Being wounded can happen when one loves the Lord, and tries their utmost to serve him. Some wounds result from unexpected loss or illness and/or etc.

Hearing a testimony of a dear lady minister that walked through illness, depression, and then dealt with all of her lost dreams made me realize how blessed I was.

If I ever was to look down my nose on the bruised and wounded—OH! please Lord allow me to see in my mind's eye the Master preparing for the garden, the cross, and washing the dirty feet of the disciples.

A young woman who I have been blessed to know, terribly disappointed her father. She became bulemic. She wrestled with this. She prayed and asked others to pray. A few years went by before she was completely delivered. She was beautiful, smar,t and she loved God beyond measure. She stayed faithful to the house of God. She worked, took care of a child, and kept believing. She got into the Word of God, and she was completely and totally healed. She came through as a child of her King. Today, she helps young girls with this issue.

A certain man from his teen years into middle age served the Lord. Unbelievable horrific chronic attacks came against him and his family. He had not been prepared for this, and he escaped into seemingly harmless things to dull life's pain. However, they gained a strong-hold on his life. His brothers and sisters in his church family prayed earnestly. The blood and the name of Jesus set him free. He is one of the most honest men I know and truly cares for others.

The family of God would have been cheated if these bruised had been given up on. Far too many believers, when wounded, will feel great loneliness. That left unattended becomes a snare. What is urgently needed is unconditional love with the Word of God. Believing in them will give new hope to carry on.

In St. John 13:34-35 we read, "A new commandment I give unto you, that you love one another, as I have loved you; By this all men will know that you are my disciples, if you have love for one another."

Those that are given love and acceptance when wounded will heal.  They shall become one who binds up the wounds for their brothers/sisters in the family of God. Perhaps you or I...!

# 26
## Farewell To The Troops

Albert and I made dream vacations on paper for years. Planning and believing we would make trips to Estes Park, Yellowstone, Myrtle Beach, and a short cruise to an island. We were blessed to make four trips to Estes Park.

The first trip was with dear friends and our pastors, Brother and Sister Davis. A few months before the trip, Albert had purchased his first and only video camera. During the trip he videoed our feet, back of heads, and then he actually filmed six hours of waterfalls. He talked non-stop the entire time at Estes Park. I, usually being a chatterbox, did not speak the first two days after arriving at Estes Park. It was as if I had been transported to where I had dreamed for years that Heidi lived. It was totally spell-binding for me. Mountains, valleys, moose, and deer so lovely it was difficult to comprehend that they were real and alive before the eyes. One of our twenty year old dreams had come true.

The time shared with Brother and Sister Davis those few days was one of the highlights of that dream vacation.

Another trip to Estes Park, Al Baby decided for us to go walking on a non-traveled trail to make a memory. Several hours into the walking memory, we had to confirm to each other that "WE ARE LOST!" As the water and snacks were gone, I was exhausted and extremely sick and fresh out of sweetness. Albert bellowed out with "We are Dying." "Huh!" was my great comeback. Al began to film my throwing up and wonderful moans. He then told me "Peaches, look into the camera and say a farewell." I was thinking, "farewell, this is what the boys and everyone will remember about me!"

A loud body of uncontrolled laughter came forth from the trees and bushes. We walked very slowly towards the sound. Right over the ridge was a group of people. That was where the laugher had come from. Their laughter was beyond what I know how to explain. The folks gave us food and water. Afterwards, they took us back to the location of where our car was.

Al Baby, by request, deleted the farewell to the troops. Well dear reader if this has not given you encouragement of the fact you and yours are really okay, then hold on.

One of our later trips to Estes Park, was with our church group in a van. Brother and Sister Davis, David,

Elaine, others, and a couple of teenagers. The Davis' were blessed by Al Baby and myself once again.

One beautiful day, Brother Davis was driving us all from Estes Park up to Mt. Evans, (a mountain with the highest paved road in North America) that was a must see for our lives. So the trip began. As I recall it was a full ninety-degree angle. Higher and higher we went up. There were no more trees anywhere. I know there were only clouds, and the angels that were with us in the van. It sunk into my thoughts, what few animals I had seen on that stairwell to heaven had all been white.

I looked out of the van window to remain calm and my eyes froze. On the right side of the van, where I was sitting, there was no road. It was directly downward for miles, with cliffs that ended in the center of the earth. I know these things: The van was near heaven's gates and ministers were in the van so the Lord would save us. The headlines flashed in my mind's eye, "Church Group Lost." The road was less narrow than before. I started declaring, "We surely are going to fall off backwards." None of the others seemed to understand. The van continued on going straight upward. "Forget these folks. They are not listening to God or me!" I was hollering. It got Brother Davis' attention. He stopped the van with only two of the wheels on this almost road. Pastor realized that I was hypervenillating! He then had someone to throw a jacket over my head. They prayed for me, got back into the van, and continued the trip to the top. Don't tell me that I won't endure to the end!

# 27
## Bob's Dealings

Bob (along with his dear wife) loves helping those who have lost their jobs, homes, and sometimes their hope.

I love the phrase the Lord cleans us up real good! Bob would tell you that applies to his life.

Bob's childhood the first few years were with his grandmother. Next he lived with his Mom and his Stepdad. During the first fifteen years there was church exposure and hearing about Jesus. At the age of twelve, he would leave home for a day or more. Bob was drinking upon turning fourteen years old. Emotional pain and the addition of emptiness were his daily emotions. Drugs love that trio.

Drugs couldn't satisfy the longing for love or give him purpose. Bob lived a blurred life and endured days and nights. Some years further down life's way, there came an opportunity to have money from drugs.

Then an interesting event started happening. During the workday, at his day job, a customer would call for business matters. The customer would insert the words "Jesus Saves". God sent the gospel in a phone message. These words tugged at Bob's heart. Thoughts lingered on those words. Somewhere in the kaleidoscope of his mind remembrances, "Jesus Saves" would emerge often. Booze, drugs, money, and being free to do his thing did not make him happy or his life worthwhile.

Twenty-nine years old and alone where he was living, Bob came to a conclusion. It was either God or death. He made a choice. He cried out unto the Lord and gave his life to Jesus.

That night, a few hours after his reaching out for help, something else happened. Bob made a second decision. He made a telephone call to the law enforcement. He gave information of upcoming dealings and happenings. They wanted to know where he was and what was he wearing. They requested to meet with him. What the outcome should entail he did not know. He just wanted to start with a totally clean slate for his life. The dealings were prevented. Bob worked for about a year in assisting to obtain information and evidence.

Bob soon began attending church. He started a long

journey towards having purpose and belonging. Bob finding help did not result in overnight happy ever after. His road has had many learning and relearning days. However, the days have had purpose and HOPE.

Sometime later, Bob found a wife and they were blessed with children.

# 28
## Al Baby Goes Home

I have done much reflecting on the days and months, before and during his departure, which were filled with many tears, miracles, and now precious memories.

Spring of 2006, Albert began to be extremely stressed. He was having headaches often. When I asked about them, he would say to me, "You are imagining this."

By the end of June, Al soon began the periods of vision problems. He fell once. I talked him into seeing his doctor. He told the doctor he was having a rough time. He scheduled to have medical tests in October 2006.

He showed mood and personality changes. He would get angry (at me) then he would change back. He could not remember any anger. He was Al Baby about one-half of the time. When he was Al Baby, he would tell me as he had for 44 years – I was his bride now, always, and forever.

Here is a thought, I do not know if there is a meaning to it or not. Albert came into to my life on a Labor Day weekend and this Labor Day weekend was the weekend that changed my life.

Albert was feeling worse than he had been. He had taken a week off (after 3 weeks of vacation) from work. Al received a call to come in, if he could. I begged him not to go to work. He insisted that he wanted to go. We shared our good byes, (that Al Baby hug and kiss). He walked around the corner of the house. I ran out the door to stop him. He was already gone. I had thoughts that filled my emotions that my life was to change forever.

Luke, our oldest grandchild, was there. The night was uneventful. I went into our bedroom, prayed, and went to bed. I knew that Albert woke me up at 11:30 to 11:34 each night for a kiss. This night I was awoke about 1:40 a.m. by Luke. He declared to me, "Grandpa is not home." I called his work. They told me that he had left work that night at the regular time.

He was two hours late. Albert was to the inch degree a person that did things in his life always at the same time. He was a person of routine. I called our sons.

Somewhere around 3:00 a.m. Al telephoned. He whispered, "I have nearly been in a car accident. I am on highway 75 (which was close to our home) and so I'll be home in a few minutes." I begged and pleaded with him to pull over and wait for Tim or Steve to come to him. His cell phone cut off. Therefore that was the end of the phone conversation. It was obvious that he was lost and he was disoriented!

Luke and Tim tried to call him over and over. Tim, I believe, got him for a few seconds and his phone battery went.

How I made it through the hours until that infamous 11:08 a.m. telephone call came, I cannot say.

Liz called. She had received a call from care flight. Al had been in a severe car wreck. No one could have prevented the accident. As soon as the impact had occurred a highway officer was able to get to the vehicle. The officer saw his uniform. The officer radioed paramedics. They arrived and had to use jaws of life to pull him out of the car. Albert was at that time transported to the nearest large hospital. It was one of those wrecks on the television news. Albert's condition was not too good.

On the phone, listening to all of this, I gathered my emotions together. Soon there were family and friends to take me to the hospital where he was. Various events transpired, confusing to my mind now. It was as if I was locked in a dark place. A place where I could not move, and I could not comprehend what was happening.

Back to the order of events on that unforgettable Monday, Labor Day of 2006. I was taken to the hospital emergency family waiting room. There were numerous friends and church family there. I was hugging some of them when an orderly came to escort me to the curtained area where my Albert was. Both of our sons were in the area. I leaned over and kissed Albert, who did not look so bad to me. How did the boys get back here so quickly? A doctor came from behind the curtain. He stood directly in front of me. He said, "Mrs. Brinkley, sit down, now!" The boys placed me in a chair as the doctor spoke. My mind understood bits and pieces of what I was being told. Albert had a tumor on his brain and spots on his liver, as well as injuries. He was to be put into the ICU unit. A neurology surgeon was called to schedule surgery. Then everything was getting fuzzy and the room was swirling.

I got up and stumbled over to Al. I began kissing him over and over. The next thing that I remember, he was in ICU and I was sitting there with him.

Within three days, he was stabilized. Steve got in touch with a well-known Dallas neuro-surgeon that had experience in brain tumors. He and the doctor made plans for the operation in two more days.

An ambulance was ordered, which transported Al, and we all went to a Dallas hospital.

I will try and tell fewer details and give you only the essence of the next four months.

Al had the brain operation. He was placed in the ICU in the large Dallas hospital. Their care was awesome for him and me. Six days blurred by. Another specialist wanted to talk with me.

Entering into the hall, in the ICU area, there was both of the boys, T.J., Jane, and James who I think had brought me. An attractive lady doctor introduced herself to me. She lead the way into a strange room. Before the door was to be closed, there was Elaine and my principal. Why are all these folks here?

I have talked to so many doctors already. They all talked as I did not have the concept of the conversations. So they must feel a woman could help me. I looked at her, then took a second look at her white coat. It had a medical tag that said cancer specialist. I remember Jane was writing down everything spoken. Our sons stayed close to me. They were touching me, I believe. The doctor began to speak about things that were going to happen to Albert. I told her that I did not want to hear anymore. I did not listen to that. She was talking about how the tumor would take his life. It was strange sounding terms. It was not going to affect Al.

Alber, knew the tumor was cancerous. He had told me. He also spoke again of the angel, the light, that came to him in the wreck. The angel said to him, "Albert, you will be alright. You are in my hands." I had the boys get me out of there right then.

Weeks after that, Albert came home. He went to a rehab unit for several hours during the daytime. He was getting so much stronger. I went and took lessons how to help him. Liz or Steve would go with me. He had seizures often at this point. He went back to the hospital for about a week in mid-November.

He would do well during the day. In the evening he then turned redfaced and would be angry. In wee hours, I would wake up and hear him praying. He prayed with peace and full of anointing. He prayed for our sons, the boys, to become close and to be there for each other. He prayed for them with supernatural faith. It was moving.

I tell most everyone that God gives us times of blessings amidst the worst trials. December 22, (our anniversary) until December 28, 2006 was a six day miracle. My Al Baby was back. Hours upon hours we held each other. We dreamed again. We prayed together, laughed together, cried together. Mostly we held each other around the clock. We prayed over and over for our children and grandchildren's futures. Thank you Lord for those days.

Mid-January 2007, Al was in total weakness once again. Seizures were nightly. One morning, he insisted that he would fix breakfast for me. He never cooked, never! Sitting down at the table, he said to me, "I am not going to fight anymore. Mary, you are past tired and I cannot go on fighting." That afternoon we had to take him to the ER once again.

While the hours went by at the emergency room, Pastor Davis was there when the Lord gave us another short miracle of time. Albert was talking to Pastor and myself. He was telling of our lives together and what it had meant to him. As usual, he was wonderful, he made me look and sound so good. I was given another memory.

Liz and Steve stayed with him and myself from then on as I recall. Their families supported them to put everyone's lives on hold.

On his trip home from the hospital, a horrible event occurred. The ambulance took him to a local nursing home instead of our house. After that emotional terror was over, we were able to get him home.

Precious times of when I got to read the Bible to him and we talked are those times I choose to remember. So many numerous times Pastor and Sister Davis were here with us.

January 29, 2007, Al raised the one arm that he still could move. "Sweet Jesus" came forth and he fell into a coma. On February 1, 2007, at 1:35 a.m. the angels came.

# 29
## The Old Lady Sub

I had began to do subbing one to two days a week for another school district.

The experience of going to different schools and finding myself being the one who knows nothing, is different for me. I had done a job for a long period of time andwas given respect. My smug little world of being in charge of a school office was now over. I show up and no longer do I size up what is needed, or even suppose to be done for that day. Thirty years ago, it was popular to go and find yourself. In the work place, I am trying to find what, who, and where I am.

My life has gone through major changes in every facet. The Lord and his angels are with me daily and nightly. However, some days I would like a cloud or pillar of fire for direction.

I'll give a good try at sharing some of the happenings

from the "Old Lady Sub" or "The Grandma Sub".

The second school I went to, I was with some Kinder-garten students. One little boy asked me, "Are you a friend of my grandma?" "No, I don't think, I know your grandma." "She is really old, too," he said.

Yesterday, I went to a classroom for one-half of the day. I was told I was to assist students with reading assign-ments. One small bit of information was omitted. These students twice daily checked in with their patrol officers.

Into the school day about forty minutes, one of the young male students (looked as he was an adult) with gang emblems tattooed on his arms, got up and declared to the room, "Be not bad to this lady. Be good for her." I thought to myself, okay. These students had sections and divided desks, of which they were not to move from. Their attempts at conning me was an art. I told them repeatedly things to help them with their work. One student blurted out with a vulgar phrase. I went to him and stated, "I do not use that kind of language, and I won't let you use it to me." The leader student then asedk me, "Have you ever had to wear a bracelet on your ankle or foot like mine?" My reply, "NO, I have not!"

The day went on with no one checking on us. I began to realize how much the Lord had been alongside of me. The leader student asked, "Do you got any kids?" "Yes, I have two sons and others that I feel are like my sons," I answered. "You are an old sub. Will you come back? You like us?" These and many more questions were asked of me. Then several of the classroom students, near the end of the day, asked, "Will you come back, and teach and tell us more?"

With these comments, I see myself in a different light. Therefore, I understand it's okay to be "The Old Lady Grandma Sub."

# 30
## The Last Word

This is the last page of this collection of stories, however it is not the end.  It is quite the opposite.

The new chapters of my story are now beginning.

NO MATTER THE AMOUNT OF SICKNESS, SUFFERING, UNFAIRNESS, GOOD TIMES, OR THE UNBEARABLE TIMES, NOTHING CAN WEAKEN GOD'S PROMISES OR HIS DESTINY IN OUR LIVES!

**WE HAVE A REASON TO CARRY ON!**

# BIOGRAPHY OF MARY JO BRINKLEY

(With Awards and Honors)

I was born on May, 1 1944 in Davenport, Iowa. My parents were Lela (Kelly) Underwood and Ernest L. Underwood. My father was killed D-Day 1944.

My maternal grandparents were a divine intervention in my caregiving and up bringing. Their role modeling and influence was nothing less than a miracle. Rev. John D. Kelly and Nellie E. Kelly, started me to church at two weeks old.

At four months of age, I had a tumor on the right side of my head near the eyes. After an operation, I was left legally blind, only 30-35% of sight. I saw only shadows of gray and klack. After several months of my family praying, and fasting, I began to see. I was healed also from a respiratory illness at 13 months old.

My family moved that year to Denison, Texas. Grandpa Kelly assisted in a church there. Five years old, I wanted so badly to go to school, to teach other kids – I told them. Grandpa talked to the ISD board. They agreed to administer and did give to me an ITBS test. I passed. I began the first grade at Cotton Mills Elementary School.

Within a year, I started to seek out parts in the different school plays. I was picked for numerous plays and made the Denison newspaper a few times. At Peabody Elementary, I won first place in 3RD GRADE READING STUDENT AWARD, AS THE TOP FOR THIRD GRADE.

My family moved to Dallas, Texas, in 1952.

Sixth grade, ten years old, I received A CERTIFICATE FOR TESTING OUT IN THE TOP 10% OF THE STATE'S READING SCORES.

Summer of 1959, I truly gave the Lord my heart, life, and future. Three weeks later my Appendix ruptured. The Lord performed a mighty healing work on my body while I was in ICU. 1960, I received the Holy Spirit, and heard of church having dramas and plays. I got deeply involved quickly. In a large church fellowship circle, I tried out and won the lead roles in several of the plays and drama sermons. I was written up in church newsletters that were sent to churches in the USA.

1961, I graduated from South Oak Cliff High School. I received a trophy for a three state Bible quiz (with adults and ministers) as well.

I attended Sherman and Dallas Business Schools. I was an excellent student in kookkeeping at both. I have had 7 college courses for business, bookkeeping and operations of several computer software. My grade point average was 3.6.

December 22, 1962, I married Albert Willington Brinkley. We have two sons, Stephen W. Brinkley and Timothy Paul Brinkley, both are married to my daughters-in-love, Karen and Liz. We have four grandchildren – Luke, Michael, Matthew and Aimee. We have one great grandchild, Emma Grace. My family is one of my greatest and best awards. I have a brother, David; and a favorite sister-in-law, Elaine, and two wonderful nieces, Michelle and Kristi.

Albert and I were married for forty-four years and forty-one days, when God called him home.

# Career and Work Achievements and or Honors

1969-1974 - Worked for the general offices of a world-wide jewelry chain. I went to work for them in one of the accounting departments.

1971- Received the honor for being the highest rated employee and produced the largest number of balanced packets in all accounting departments. Promoted twice and was offered another promotion.

1976 - Began to work for Dallas ISD. Started out as a reading assistant.

1977 - Promoted to a library clerk. Within one year moved to a level two clerk.

1980 - Promoted to a principal's clerk. Moved up three steps the next year and began to do the school ledgers.

1983 - Promoted to school secretary

1985- Requested by administration to join the Superindent's Spoke Group for secretaries. This was a high honor.

1986 -Given the "Life-Time Member Award of Outstanding Achievement for School Employees" from the State of Texas and The Texas State PTA's.

1987 - Named one of the finalists in the Apple Award for Highly Excellent School Secretaries.

1987 - Chosen for Positive Parent Award for Dallas ISD secretaries.
1991 - Dallas newspaper wrote a couple of pieces on me, highlighting School Secretaries.

1991- Another newspaper write up for assisting a principal with the new concept to the elementary school for parents committee SCE.

1997 - Dallas Association of Education Office Personnel selected me for the "Outstanding Secretary Service Award"

1988 - Newspaper article on for the Dallas Schools "Secretary of Quality and Excellence" they wrote how elementary school secretaries were among the hardest working employees. They told about me and quoted me throughout the piece.

1994 -1995 - Requested to assist in creating a new elementary secretaries manual, trained new secretaries, and helped secretaries in organizing school offices.

1998 - Honored at the Dallas Educational Clerical Workers Assocation annual luncheon, with Highest Leadership award with others.

2001 - One of the first few school secretaries to become recognized as Texas Highly Qualified Office Managers.

2008 -Chambridge Who's Who Among Americas' Women Executives/ the Professional Education Executives division chose me to be honored and to be included in their next book, Honors of American Women Edition.

2008 - RETIRED

# Church Awards and Achievements:

1973 – 1983  Wrote short stories for a church denominational newsletter.

1974 - 1978  Created a puppet duo with Judy Coggins, "A Bird and Miss Sunshine." Wrote and created stories for children and performed in numerous churches in Texas. Re wrote Sunday School cirrculum for the 1st-3rd graders and used live Bible characters to teach these programs.

1978-1992 -Wrote, directed, and delivered eleven messages of illustrated sermons, assisted by high school students. Ministered these illustrated sermons at Youth Rallies and Conferences in other cities.

1979 -Won in a Church Association tri-state Youth Conference for the best youth ministry presented. The entire Youth Groups from those different churches presented me with the awards given. The association presented me with a Mary Jo Day and luncheon.

1977-1992 - Taught high school Sunday School classes. Every two years we covered the Epistles. I gave a test on the subject matter. I had the young people to teach lessons on the subject as a part of their exam. I also gathered students to my home for small group prayer and socials.

2009-2010 - The Lord has used me often in a new area, such as in restaurants, drug stores, neighborhood driveways, fellow workers cars, and to interrupt ISD training sessions (at break periods) to pray with others and give words of encouragement.

I could have not done any of these things, natural or spiritual, without the Lord and all the love and prayers for me. There are so many others that have blessed my life .

# Notes